HUMAN EMOTIONS
A   Book   Of   Poetry

KATHLEEN TAYLOR-BENNETT

authorHOUSE™

1663 LIBERTY DRIVE, SUITE 200
BLOOMINGTON, INDIANA 47403
(800) 839-8640
WWW.AUTHORHOUSE.COM

First published by AuthorHouse 12/09/05

ISBN: 1-4259-0396-7 (sc)

Printed in the United States of America
Bloomington, Indiana

This book is printed on acid-free paper.

I would like to dedicate this book to my mother, Ann Hall, and my father, the late John Lincoln Taylor, my two brothers Dexter (Penny P) Hall of Portland Ore and Clarence (Elsie) Hall of Tallulah, La; my seven sisters Threasa Hall, Jovita Hall, Perri (James) Johnson, Traci Heath, Erica Taylor and Johnni Taylor all of Vicksburg, Ms and Gwendolyn Hogan of Jackson, Ms along with my many nieces and nephews.

A special dedication goes out to my husband, Anthony C Bennett Sr. and our children Sheann A Taylor, Anthony C Bennett Jr. and Taylor J Bennett of Vicksburg, I love you all more than you could ever know.

To my best friends and sisters, Natasha Derby-West of Vicksburg and Kimberly Smith-Turner of Atlanta Ga., Thank you for being you!

A WOMAN'S PRAYER

Now I lay me down to sleep
I pray for a man that will not creep
I pray to have an honest trust
That he will not cheat in spite of lust
I pray he holds respect for me high
And not begin the cycle of lies
I pray he knows what he has in me
Because what he doesn't, another will see
I pray to find this all in one man
Because finding a good one is like sifting through sand

ABDUCTED VOICE

Why isn't it alright that I say what I feel
My voice is my outlet, it helps me to heal
It helps me make sense of my emotions inside
I say it, I feel it, and move on with stride
You try and silence it with spiteful overtones
But I will not be silenced, I have done nothing wrong
My voice is my savior, my strength, and my friend
I will use it forever, over and over again

ACCEPTING THE WORSE

I knew she told my business
But she was the only one that would listen
I knew the relationship was bad
But without it I had nothing at all
I knew the grass was greener on the other side
But I wasn't use to not having to mow
I knew it wasn't any good
But it was all I could afford
I knew it didn't pay well
But I had to take whatever came along
I knew my chances weren't good
But I had to take the risk and try anyway
With all the paths I could have taken
I chose to continue to be mistaken

AFTER THE RAIN

Today it rained, I feel no peace
I'm not happy at all, not in the least
I don't know what happened, I used to be happy
Now I fuss, I scream, I'm always snappy
I feel as if there's a hole in my heart
The world won't let me in, I play no part
If I dig a whole and just crawl in
Maybe all this uncertainty will end
When I close my eyes at night to sleep
I feel held down, confined, in too deep
I don't know why I feel this pain
I pray it will end After The Rain

AFTERLIFE

Through man's evil eyes
I see our worlds demise
In the blackness of his heart
I see us torn apart
With the wickedness in his voice
He takes away our right of choice
With the hate that rolls from his tongue
Because of our differences-from each other we shun
But god is almighty and a force to be reckoned
A peaceful world for his, to it he will see
That all living in his grace
Will rejoice with thee
In a world without sick and free of sin
With happiness in sight and to it no end

AFTERWORLD

Like no other place I've ever been
The soft brisk winds brush against my skin
The birds are chirping, the water is clean
This place is filled with wonder, it's so serene
Walking in wonder this place is like
Dancing in heaven, seeing the light
I move around without a care
Living as if I'm one with the air
I live in this place only in my mind
But will be there one day
At that predetermined time!

AIN'T IT FUNNY

Ain't it funny
When you go so far
To have gone nowhere at all
Ain't it funny
When you do so much
To have done nothing at all
Ain't it funny
When you learn so much
And yet, have learned nothing at all
Ain't it funny
When you've loved so much
To have gotten no love at all
Ain't it funny
When you try so hard
And still end up
Against a brick wall

ALL ABOUT YOU

You only come around when YOU need
What about me, do I count, don't I bleed?
Did you ask how I was or if I needed to talk?
How about if I needed to exhale, to take a walk?
Oh, I forgot; it's all about you
Did you ever stop and wonder how one-sided this is?
My problems are of no concern to you, only his
What if I weren't here to lift YOU up?
If I said I'm done, would you call my bluff?
I have problems and need a shoulder sometimes too
Oh, I forgot; it's all about you
You'll go days, weeks, and months without a word
I've been through so much, some you haven't heard
One day you will wake up and see
There's more to this friendship than you, there's also ME

ALL OF THIS

For your love, honor, respect and mind
You can have my body, heart, soul and time
I'll give you these things of my free will
If you accept them honestly from now until
The end of time that you and I
Will be together until the day we die

AND THEN THERE WERE NONE

From the time we met, I knew that I
Would love you forever, until the day we die
I put so much into what we had
Because as long as I had you, not a day would I be sad
We grew so much from the love we shared
And spent time with our hearts because we cared
But one day you let go and forced a wedge
Between you and I and the love that we pledged
The feelings we had died one by one
They left without struggle until there were none

ANECDOTE ... MY LIFE

Let me tell you how I came to be
The person inside that I call me
I struggled to earn my right to this
But managed victory because of a twist
My ups and downs had taught me well
They showed me how to soften a hard sell
I found that once I walked inside
The people I met would join my stride
I allowed them to talk and walk my thoughts
And showed them our strengths are born from our faults

APOSTASY

The reason behind it is still unclear
Was it because I allowed it
Or because I didn't care
Should I have trusted my instincts
Or lived through the lesson as I did
Shame on me for not being stronger
Shame on you for taking advantage
I'm ashamed because I was weak
I'm stronger because I finally stood up
Whatever the reason
I'm a better person because it made me tough

ASK AND YOU SHALL RECEIVE

Ask for his love
He'll brighten your day
Ask him for direction
He won't lead you astray
Ask him for guidance
He hears what you say
Give him your pain
He'll take it away
Show him you're willing to live life his way
And with each of his blessings comes another day

BACK ROADS

My heart is aching
I feel so much pain
Choking on my thoughts
Trying to sustain
Crying over my memories
Sifting through regret
Remembering all the things done wrong
Trying to forget
Wasting away in anguish
Losing who I was
Feeding on self doubt
Living in a glove

BEAUTIFUL

Beauty is in the eye of the beholder
She knew she was beautiful
Though no one ever told her
She wasn't overly cute or very thin
But she's beautiful inside, down within
She was very helpful and had a big heart
If she was going to be beautiful
She knew that caring was the start
She didn't need attention to feel this way
She reminded herself each and every day
So if you don't fit the stereotype on TV
Remember that within the truth you will see
You are beautiful if you feel it in your soul
And if you feel it, your beauty will show

BECAUSE HE ALLOWS

I wake each morning
And face my fears
Because I'm never alone
And he always hears
When I call out for his
Guidance and grace
He steadies my hand
And renews my faith
He keeps me level
And helps me to see
What I have in him
And what his joy is to be
He clears the path
And walks with me
To that place where his
Is all I need

BECAUSE OF HIM

I wake every day
And take a breath
Without him replenishing
I have none left
I'm guided everyday
Through his sight
When the world takes
He makes it right
He shows me the good
In all the bad
And that I don't need
What I once had
If it were meant
It would be here
What was once foggy
Is now so clear
I now appreciate my life as it is
Because I'm living it in accordance
With his

BEFORE AND AFTER

Men say they love us and they would give us the world
Once they get us they treat us like any common girl
Before, they're grateful to shower us with gifts
After, their attitudes become cold and stiff
Before, they could care less if ten inches they pinch
After, they won't come within an inch
Before, their words so soft and sweet
After, getting them to acknowledge you is a feat
Before, they said, "I love you" with a smile
After, they act as if saying it puts them on trial
Before, they would do just about anything you ask
After, they do nothing, removing what was once their mask
Take a picture so you can capture
The difference you'll see in their before and after

BEFORE YOU SPEAK

Sometimes I must think before I speak
It's easy to say and do things in a moment of heat
People often say things because they don't care
The smart thing to do is to act as if they aren't there
They talk behind your back and put you down
Have lies spread about you all over town
You have to be strong and brush it off
You won't last at all if your feelings are too soft
I often wonder why people waste their time
Not living their lives, trying to live mine
So if things get bad and you get weak
Just take a moment and think before you speak

BELIEF

Healing may take a while
But I know you're here with me
Taking longer than I think it should
But you know how long it has to be
Me learning from it all
You teaching me with your all
Going through the ups and downs
You keeping my feet on the ground
Thoughts spinning in my head
You holding on to my heart
Me remembering from beginning to end
You giving me another start

BETRAYAL

He cheated on me, he broke my heart
Turned my world inside out, tore it apart
I asked him why he did it; he said he doesn't know why
I could slap his face for telling me that lie
I cooked, I cleaned, and I gave him kids
I can't imagine why he would do what he did
I want to leave him but I love him too much
I can't deal with the lies, the hurt, it's too much
Forever trust is gone; there can be no more
He lost the respect I had for him because he needed to score
I don't know what will happen, how this will end
He lost what he had in me, his lover, his friend

BLACK

Slendering to the eye
Seductive to the mind
Mysterious to the soul
Color of liquid gold
Intriguing to the unknown
Beautiful to all shown
Harder for those born in it
Proud of being it
Overcoming stigma
Beauty like no other

BORROWED LOVE

He belonged to her; he was not free
I wanted him to leave and be with me
We would spend time while she was at work
We knew if she found out it would cause her to hurt
He committed his heart and soul to her
But he broke all his promises and let our affair occur
The time had now come to make him choose
One of us would be sad because someone would lose
My heart is blind to what my eyes can see
He's never going to leave her and be with me

BOTTLED UP

You're a filthy, lying piece of snake in the grass trash
I hope the slut gives you a nasty rash
I hope she takes you for every dime you have
And leave you with not even enough for a cab
Then you can choke on all the lies you told
And burn in hell with your wretched soul

BRANCHES

Growing up and sprouting out
Feeding on self hate and doubt
Breaking off to grow a new
Way to loathe and despise you
Bending from wind of angry thoughts
Striking the face of the one that taught
Me to trust and give a chance
To the man that planted my circumstance
Uprooting my life with disarray
Burying the seeds for another day

BREAKDOWN

Leaving for me was the right thing to do
But how in the hell can I live without you
In the middle of nowhere wanting to turn back
Having with me only a suitcase and a sack
Crying the tears of letting go
Dragging my feet like I'm on death row
Reaching the end of this dead end town
Praying for strength that I don't breakdown

BREAKFAST

It helps me to determine my morning
And whether or not the day will be tormenting
Orange juice going down is like a smooth day
Keeping the headaches and troubles at bay
Cereal is the multi-tasking that has to be done
Guaranteeing the day is no fun
Toast is like the crisp morning air
Waking me up, giving me that flair
Oatmeal is like warming of the soul
Pushing me to attain my goals
Grits and eggs are the perfect combination
Filling me up, boosting sensations
With any of the above I have to choose
My morning coffee, can't afford to snooze!

CARE-FREE

Through heavens starry eyes
I see the bright moon shine
With his wide open arms
I feel the sun and all it's warm
Through grassy plains that stretch for miles
I soar my oats and all their wilds
With clean fresh air that takes my breath away
I'm thankful for it's touch each and every day
With the downpour of rain I weep and cry
But as the rain dries, so does each eye
And as the sun sets, I learn that I too
Must prepare for the next chapter
So he can walk me through

CHOICES

I got so mad today at work
I met someone I wanted to hurt
She looked at me with a wicked grin
I wanted to hit her, to kick her, to sin
She came to the counter to pick at me
Oh how I wanted to make her bleed
She asked me a question with hate in her voice
If I do it, I'm not sorry, it was her choice
I answered her question with a smile on my face
Her anger was obvious, my blood she could taste
I decided not to play her stupid game
If I let her push my buttons, I would be to blame
She seem to be shocked, bewildered, amazed
I took the high road and she got played
In the real world there are no voices
We're each responsible for our choices

CLOSENESS

What I need
When I'm feeling alone
What I need
When I'm no longer strong
What I need
When I'm feeling dark
What I need
When I'm falling apart
What I need
When I'm trying to be
Something other than just me

COME FLY WITH ME

Come fly with me
I'm in no hurry
Come fly with me
Give me your worries
Come fly with me
Let's taste the rain
Come fly with me
I'll take away your pain
Come fly with me
Be one with the air
Come fly with me
Where you need to be
I'll take you there
Come fly with me
Give me your plight
Come fly with me
It is now my fight
Come fly with me
Give your life to me
Come fly with me
Joy eternally

CONDEMNATION OF ME

Stillness of my heart
Images in my mind
Bewilderment of my soul
They're gripping me, troubled times
Breeze of tainted air
Memories causing despair
Love, the feel of bee stings
Shattering all my dreams
Two steps I move forward
Ten steps he pushes me back
To live I need to breathe
My oxygen he holds, I lack
Drowning in myself
Dying a thousand times
Trying to free myself
From the cage within my mind

CONSISTENCY

Being true to yourself is a task all its own
Trying to please other people to feel not so alone
Day in day out nothing for you
People taking things the wrong way
Trying to misconstrue
You give and you give until there's no more
Being held down not able to spread your wings and soar
From sun up till sun down you do for everyone else
Forgetting about what you need
And not taking time for yourself
It's time to look out for you and stand your ground
Regardless to what you say or do
Someone will always have a frown
It's time to take heed and be whom you want to be
All it takes is a little courage and some consistency

COUNTRY HOME

It was old and run down
It was new and breathtaking
It was a place of loneliness and sadness
It was my place of peace and joy
Many years it was there
Not enough years had it been
Remembering
Birds singing as the sun rose
And crickets chirping as it set
The hours in between are long and endless
The minutes short and sweet
Time is playing tricks on my eyes
Memories setting up shop in my heart

CURIOSITY

I know you've been with her and me
What you do in the dark my eyes still see
Going back and forth from there to here
What you whisper to her my ears will hear
Do you think it's fun the games you play
What if I treated you the same way
Are you in love with your lady friend
Or is this just fun at my expense
After all our years of hard earned trust
Why throw it away for the thrill of cheap lust
At the end of the day when you're done with play
Does she love you as much as I do everyday

DEADPAN EYES

Still and dark
Without shine or glare
Looking into life
With a burdened stare
Rolling without movement
Eyes circling the room
Searching their souls
For that date with doom
Seeing right through
Their chaste disguise
Digging a hole
With emotionless eyes

DELIRIUM

Seeing shadows that are not there
Feeling with eyes that only stare
Longing for what is not to be
Begging with a silent plea
Spinning in a backwards motion
Thinking without a definite notion
Hearing what has not yet been said
Turmoil chaotic within my head
Settling into a wayward wrath
Forgetting to distance me from my past

DEPRECATION OF LIFE

It's never good and always unfair
I live it with overwhelming despair
I seem to be cursed with such bad luck
Twisting and turning, running amok
The pleasures of it have passed me by
My heart now only know's to despise
I'm tired of living this day-to-day fight
It feels life is given solely out of spite

DESERT WINDS

You and I hand in hand
Walking back in time through sand
Reviewing memories of our time together
Wishing it could have lasted forever
Skipping past the hurt and pain
Drying the tears from our time in the rain
Cherishing past moments with family and friends
Wondering why it came to an end
Confident that we will see them again
Once we get through the desert winds

DISTORTED RELEASE

I've broken away and I'm finally free
But forgot where it was I used to be
For this time I have forever longed
But I seem to have misplaced
What I remember as home
From my troubles I have turned away
But my pain seems set to stay
I'm rid of the chains and shackles of him
But feel disdainfully depraved and grim
I've turned my back on shadows of the past
And am no longer a part of his sadistic cast

DROWNING

Under myself and I can not breathe
Too far over myself to be at ease
Sinking in the thickness of a troubled mind
Turning counter clockwise fighting time
Seeing through eyes that demolish with sight
Just holding on to life has become my plight

EMPLOYERS

They tell us that we're doing so good, giving all types of praise
But somehow we're never doing good enough to get that raise
They tell us we're appreciated and that we can't be replaced
But as soon as something goes wrong they rush to judge in haste
We like our jobs and the money, but if you think about it, it's almost funny
We do so much to show our loyalty to them
But every Christmas season, bonus time, they cry budget trims
It's hard to get a day off or even take a break
But they wonder why it's possible for you to make a mistake
I can't be the only one that would like to place an order
For a new, a more generous, long term employer

EVIDENCE

It was there all the time
I saw it, but pretended to be blind
I thought if I looked away
It would disappear
But the harder I tried to ignore it
The more it became clear
I was too afraid to confront it
I tried but always faltered
My eyes were refusing to see
What was obviously best for me
This lie was my truth
The truth I'd always known
Anything else I saw
I had refused to own
It's a sign of weakness for me
Trying to make myself believe
It is easier to live in pretence
Than face overwhelming evidence

FELLOWSHIP WITHIN

I am my partner
I am my friend
I am my soul mate
I am my kin
I am my backbone
I am my shoulder
I am my strength
I am my soldier
I am my thoughts
I am my feelings
I am my prayer
I am my healings
I am everything I have been
I am my fellowship within

FORGIVENESS

It takes a lot but we must try
To let ill feelings wither and die
Anger takes so much from who we are
Cutting us deep, leaving a scar
Our minds are filled with hate and revenge
It's been so long but we won't let it end
It plays over and over keeping it fresh
Rotting our hearts to the smell of dead flesh
You say that in order for you to live
You have to loathe and refuse to forgive
But in order to move on there must be a willingness
To give up hate in exchange for forgiveness

FREEDOM

Walking without hurry
Living without worry
Sleeping without fear
Loved ones near and dear
Food on the table
Working because you're able
Peace around the world that lasts
War a distant memory of the past
Shaking the hand of your fellow man
Proud to be an American

FRIENDSHIP

Simple to the soul
Warm to the heart
There when you need it
Never growing apart
Asking what you need
Never feeling envy
Far from feeling tiresome
Helpfulness flowing plenty
More valuable than a diamond
It cannot be replaced
Living life without it
Would surely be a waste

GOODBYE

It was fun while it lasted but it's come to a close
We're both going down the paths we chose
We knew from the beginning we didn't have a chance
There's no need for us to take that last glance
We fought letting go for far too long
We can't be friends because we're both prone
To start it back up hoping to be
More than we can and we both see
That saying it's over is the best thing for us
There's no need for words because we'd only fuss
About who was right and who was wrong
Going over and over the same ol' song
The time has come and there's no need to try
All we have to do is just say "goodbye"

HAPPINESS

Inside my mind
Far from my heart
Visible to my eyes
Just out of my grasp
Next to me
Many miles away
Down the same path
Going opposite ways
Living within me
Unable to be felt
Though it speaks aloud
I cannot hear it
Circling my soul
Eluding my spirit
Not much longer will I have to seek
I owe myself that part of me

HER FOREVER GIVING

Dedication: my mother, Anester (Ann) Hall

When she had, we had
When she didn't, hearts sad
When she couldn't, it burned
But because she tried, times turned
Encouragement came with a smile
Desperation deep all the while
Privilege living a state away
Hardship fighting to take our plates
Determination wide as the sea
Trying to quiet each silent plea

Her name is TEMPTATION

With sinister eyes
She lured him in
With poisonous lips
She teased his ears
With her sensual touch
She heated his flesh
With weakness of mind
He failed the test
Within the evil of her web
He gave in to sin
With the break of day
He vowed to never do it again
But it was too late for him
To change his mistake
And now with great anger
"He" will judge his fate

HERMETIC HEART

You can't get in, I will not share
The thing within that makes me care
I will not open it up to you
And watch my feelings beat grey and blue
I've felt the pain that goes along with
Giving yourself to form a fit
I learned my lesson from the start
And now feel safe within my hermetic heart

HUSBAND

"To Anthony, I Love You"

You are my lifeline
You hold me together
You come to my rescue
Whatever the weather
You open the doors
When I slam them shut
You tend to my wounds
When I cut myself up
You shut out the sound
To stop the screams
You enter my mind
To suppress evil dreams
You open my eyes
To show me the light
You guide my journey
When I'm lost in the night
I'm never alone
You're always with me
My lover, my friend
My everything

IF ONLY

Today I looked him in the eyes
My heart pounding, but I could not lie
He said he loved and wanted to be with me
I cried because I wanted to be free
I told him my feelings for him had passed
The look on his face, I felt so sad
Our life had been so ugly together
Tragically, a storm we could not weather
He asked if time would change my mind
But pain of the past has yet to subside
We took the wrong turns in life before
And I wasn't willing to do it anymore
Together we've lived so miserably
Apart we're sure to be at ease
I said goodbye and walked away
Hoping his pain will ease one day

IF WE KISSED

Longing to touch you
The need in me
To be in your arms
To hear you breathe
To smell your cologne
To feel your breath
All over my body
All restraint away swept
The look in your eyes
The beat of your heart
Your lips close to mine
It's too late not to start

IN YOUR EYES

I see my future and I've lost all my pain
I'm in from the cold and out of the rain
There are no more clouds; there are only blue skies
You accept me for who I am inside
You bring me joy and show me love
You're always beside me and never above
I'm no longer living with foolish pride
Because I see my world in your eyes

INEVITABLE SURRENDER

I cried and paced around the room
The time had come to meet with doom
It came to collect my broken soul
I wasn't ready, my story hadn't been fully told
I pleaded and tried to extend my time
It refused and took hold of my mind
I fought at first but soon gave in
It's taken over me; my story will have no end

INSECURITIES

Am I jealous because I "think" she's cuter than me
Or insecure because of what you did to me
Do you think her body's better than mine
Or should I not worry because we have a family and time
Do I think you'd ever leave me for her
Or should I believe no such thing would ever occur
Do you badmouth me behind my back
Or is your respect for me solid and intact
Will you cheat if I'm not with you
Or remember your vows to me and hold them true
Should I worry that I'm not the girl I used to be
Or believe you love me as your woman faithfully
When all is said and done do I have your word that you
Will remember that I am your woman, your friend
Always walking beside you

INSPIRATION

It comes from within
It comes when you're without
It's there when you're strong
It's there when you're in doubt
It's there to hold your hand
It's there to show that you can
It's there to hold you up
It's there to insure you never give up

INTENTIONAL MISTAKE

Why did you do it
You knew it was wrong
Again you've been caught
Singing the same ol' song
"I'm sorry I did it
It won't happen again"
Same thing you said
When you did it with my friend
Begging and weeping
With crocodile tears
When will this stop
This has been going on for years
I'm tired of your games
I won't play them anymore
The field is now level
And it's my turn to score

JUST LIKE YOU

I'm not like you, atleast I try not to be
But I'm just like you, even while trying to be me
I walk in your shoes and follow your stride
I lie about my faults and my shame I try to hide
I often wonder why I criticize you
When not even I know how to be true
You talk about people and I jump in and add
I'm just as pitiful as you, our lives are so sad
When the tables are turned however, our attitudes are cad
We are quick to get defensive and so very mad
I guess I stick around because I know it to be true
That you will stick with me because I'm just like you

K A R M A

What you did to me I'm going to do to you
The pain I felt you're going to feel it too
The lies you told and I believed
Have taught me how in turn to deceive
I'm going to smile up in your face
While planning on someone taking your place
I'm going to lead you by a string
While continuing my extra-marital fling
I hope this eats you to the core
When I decide to walk out of the door

LET GO

Waking up to breathe new air
After the demise of a relationship full of despair
Opening your eyes to see the light
After the torturous thoughts
That troubled you through the night
Focusing your ears to hear the sounds
Of a new beginning coming around
Tasting the sweetness of another day
Letting go of the troubles of yesterday
Feeling the beat of a reborn heart
Anxious for life with a brand new start

L O S E R

When I see you I'm always nervous and tense
You laugh and make jokes at my expense
You make things hard on me everyday
I gave you no reason to treat me this way
I've never done anything mean to you
But you treat me as if you don't have a clue
That the things you say hurt my pride
And the things you do kill me inside
When I close my eyes at night to sleep
I pray they do not reopen to have some peace
But they always do and I'm forced again
To relive the humiliation and not defend
Myself against this torture and pain
Because I'm not part of the game

LOST

I can't get over it
I can't move on
My heart is heavy
My soul now stone
My memories twisted
My mind is stressed
Our love is gone
My life's a mess

L O V E

In it you feel it
Outside it you see it
Seeing it you want it
Wanting it you go after it
Close to it you sense it
With someone you share it
Abused it you damage it
Neglect it you lose it
Away from it you miss it
Alone you long for it
Deny it you'll never have it!

LOVE GONE AWAY

Not enough years we had together
So much love we had for each other
Never did life pass us by
And yet we still had to say goodbye
Our family had grown from two to five
If only we had been given more time
To do all the things we did again
I wish your life didn't have to end
Though I'm grateful for my time with you
It was over and gone far too soon

MEANT TO BE

Through your eyes, my future I see
I feel in your heart, our destiny
Though the curves are winding
And the roads can be long
With us making the effort
Strengthens our home
Though our battles sometimes
Move uphill
Looking into each others eyes
Time stands still
With you by my side
My worries seem few
And our patience and love
Keeps us true

MELANCHOLY

Feeling lost and far away
Sad and meandered with the light of day
Conscious but struggling to stay afloat
Poisoned and holding the antidote
Twisting without hope to save my life
Weak because I have lost all fight
Falling without a hand to hold
Turning my back on my dying soul

MEMORIES YET TO COME

Traveling forward in my mind
Sifting through untold time
Seeing it the way I want it to be
Tangled within defined mystique
Circling around, in and out
Future memories becoming my clout
Turning around to return home
From places deep within my unknown

MIRACLES

It's the healing to our sickness
The light to our darkness
It's the sight to our blindness
Every act of kindness
It's the sun to our rain
The warmth to our cold
It's the answer to our prayers
The hand we can hold
It's the truth we can trust
The right to our wrongs
It's everything that is possible
When we believe, what we are shown

M I S E R Y

I find myself in total gloom
Pacing back and forth in this small room
I try and convince myself I'm gonna be ok
But find myself tired and dismayed
I wonder how this day will end
Hoping to talk with a family member or friend
Yesterday was bad, today is worse
My only hope is to get down on my knees
And pray to end this curse
I'll trust in god and try to believe
Some day, some how, I'll be rid of this misery

M I S F I T

I didn't belong and could not stay
My life had turned an awkward way
I rummaged around for my place in this
But found no solution, I did not fit
I didn't know how to live within
A society in which I did not blend
I packed myself to turn and leave
So that I may finally be at ease

M Y F A T H E R

Dedication: My father, John L. Taylor

What he did for me I can never repay
It didn't take money or gifts for me to be able to say
My father was a good man dear to my heart
He was gone before I felt we had a start
He taught me to love and look out for myself
And that I can be happy with little or no wealth
His eyes were intense and heart was pure
Living without him is like a disease with no cure
I know he's in a better place and I'll see him again
Until then I bow my head, thank the lord, and say
Amen

MY INTERNAL GRAVE

Deep down inside of me
I know I'm the person I want to be
Why do I feel so stressed and alone
With a hardened heart, solid as stone
I cry and wonder could it be
I've lost all hope, my life, my sanity
I reach out to help anyone in need
I get nothing in return, it cuts, I bleed
My soul feels trapped, lonely, and exposed
It's like my life, planned out, has been transposed
I know if I walk forward and hold my head high
My hopes and dreams will again soar high as the sky
If I don't control these feelings, I can't be saved
I'll continue to walk blindly within
My internal grave

MY LOVING ANGEL

In loving memory: Michael Jay Jackson Jr.

With subtle warning and without fear
You've traveled far away and yet so near
You said goodbye on the day of your birth
You breathed your last breath along with your first
You stayed long enough for us to learn
That our place in heaven, we will have to earn
Though your body was weak, your spirit was strong
Only here for a short while, awaiting your return home
It was as it was meant and we loved you strong
But we had to let go so you can return where you belong
With intense pain and heavy hearts
We accepted that you played a much bigger part
In showing us what we take for granted
That seed in us you have securely planted
And until the day we see you again
We'll hold your memory close, deep within

MY MINDS VERSION

I didn't believe it, it couldn't be true
That your entire conversation was about me and you
She stood too close and smiled too much
The look in your eyes, you wanted to touch
You sat and talked for hours on end
I know she was more than just your friend
You bought her drinks and paid for her food
The look in her eyes, she was in the mood
I was going crazy, I was becoming a fiend
All because of this stupid dream

MY TURN

Who do you think you are fussing at me?
Because I'm no longer blind and my eyes now see
You're a liar, a cheat, a toad, and a dog
You had me confused with my head in a fog
You did me wrong and I said nothing at first
But you would surely die now if I had to quench your thirst
Because I see you now for what you are
A disgusting little boy whom I will now see from afar
It took a long time but I finally learned
You're done spinning the wheel and now it's my turn

ON BENDING KNEES

Can you hear me
I know you can
You hear the plea
Of every man
I ask for direction
You show me the way
I ask for light
You give another day
I pray for healing
You ease my pain
To quench my thirst
You give me rain
When hope is lost
You help me to see
That you hear all cries
On bending knees

ONE DAY

Sometimes I think life just isn't fair
Like no one listens and no one cares
I try and do right but cannot believe
All the bad things that happen to me
I lost my spouse, my family, my job
All I want to do is break down and sob
I know I have to be positive and strong
Things will turn around for me again before long
I can't do anything stupid because I can't take it back
I'll have to live with that knowledge, that awful fact
Until things get better, I'll continue to pray
That life is good for me again one day

ONE TO TEN

Once was not enough
Twice, you messed things up
Three times you said never again
Four times, you intentionally sinned
Five times you played the field
Six times, wounds that will not heal
Seven times without your ring
Eight times, just another fling
Nine times another lie
Ten times, I said goodbye

OUR LIFE

I'm never out and always home
Never with you and always alone
You never hold my hand or say that you
Will love me always regardless to
What the world sends our way
We were meant to be and will always stay
True to each other because we care
About what we have been given in life to share

PAINTED

The colors of the world are bold and true
Taking on different shapes and sizes becoming anew
We each are different in our own special way
Hopefully lighting a candle for peace each and every day
The troubles of the world make it prominent and stained
Shackling us down keeping us detained
What we do to each other out of anger and hate
Keeps us divided and determines all our fate
If we all set aside our differences and keep our minds from being tainted
The world would flourish with togetherness so beautifully painted

PARADISE

A place where I can be me
A place where all are free
A place where nothing costs
A place where there's never a loss
A place of breathtaking beauty
A place free of active duty
A place of rainbow flowers
A place of light rain showers
A place with miles of glee
A place for every fantasy
A place that always insists
On pure and plentiful bliss

PEACE

I feel it within me
I know it's there
I want to take hold
It avoids my glare
It eludes my grasp
But hears my calls
There's no response
As darkness falls
For it I've beseeched
Day in day out
It turns and run
As I scream and shout
It shows me the way
But I miss each turn
It's teaching a lesson
But I fail to learn
It's waiting for me
All I have to do is want
To catch up to it
And hold on taut

PERSONAL FOOL

Can I wash your clothes and cook your food
I'll even clean your house and adjust to your moods
I'll take out the trash and cut the grass
Wash the cars and even kiss your ass
I'll work two jobs and pay the bills
Run all your errands with time to kill
I'll never get angry or lose my cool
I'm here for you...I'm your personal fool

PHASES

Is it ever a good or bad day
Or just not the day you would have chosen
Do you need to have those things
Or does time, without them, seem to be frozen
Should I be unhappy with my life
Or be appreciative that I am alive
Do I really dislike this person
Or is what I see a reflection of me
Could I have done something more
Or was what I did more than enough
Should I stay and fight for what's mine
Or walk away, if it's mine it will come
At the end of the day am I happy with me
Or disappointed that what I am.. I will be

PIECES OF ME

In your eyes
By your side
On your mind
Forever in time
Part of your soul
Til' the age of old
In your heart
Never apart

PITIFUL BOY

You gave her money
You crossed the line
I'd rather you shared
Your pitiful ass time
You took from me
You took from the kids
You're not even man enough
To admit what you did
Now you're scrambling
To cover your ass
This relationship of ours
Is not going to last
I'm sick of you doing
This shit to me
I wish you would just get out
And leave me the hell be

POETRY

My life
My fears
My blood
My tears
My laughs
My cries
My lows
My Highs
My love
My hate
My destiny
My fate
My memories
My choice
My anger
My voice
My moods
My flings
My everything

QUICKSAND

Sinking within myself
Drowning deep in sorrow
Motionless with fear
My cries no one can hear
Swallowing my soul
Sucking me up whole
Happiness gone I'm stuck
My time is almost up

PONDERING

Sometimes I wonder if I should have left
Started thinking about happiness for myself
We have so many years and so much history
The last ten years for us though, have been a mystery
He doesn't know what I want or need
He's running out of time and better take heed
I have to again start living for myself
Take time for me, forget everyone else
I love him dearly and don't want to be a quitter
But I'd rather find happiness than to be bitter
I know he'll understand because even he can see
The problems recurring between him and me

RE-ACTIONS

What would you do if I gave you a chance
If I would give you that second glance
Would you come to me and put out your hand
Introducing yourself like a real man
Or would you come with some tired line
Making a fool of yourself, wasting my time
I hope you would not choose the latter
Because anything else you said wouldn't matter
You see a woman like me commands respect
Any man not giving it would surely regret
Having come up to me in the first place
Making a bad decision in a moment of haste
What so many of you fail to see
Is that a real woman won't be taken so easily
I have to know what's on your mind
If you're really worth any of my time
So before you leap, think about your actions
Because for every one I have a re-action

REAL WOMEN

We are their backbones, we hold them up
We keep things calm when it gets rough
We cook, we clean and take care of the kids
We also hold jobs, we will no longer be hid
We also pay bills and balance the books
We're finally getting our respect
Oh, how very long it has took
We're no longer walking behind them
Those days are over
If we can't walk beside them, we'll just bulldozer
Things will be equal from here on out
There's no need to pout with anger and shout
We make our own way, nothing has to be given
We are the new breed, we are real women

REDEMPTION

They said I couldn't do it
I had to prove them wrong
They said I was too weak
I proved I was strong
They said I lacked ambition
That I didn't know what I wanted
I reached high, grabbed hold
And when I owned it, I flaunted
Once I'm sure what I want
I have no problem achieving it
Now they have to look at me, open wide, and eat it!

REFLECTIONS

You walk around with your nose in the air
Whispering about people like you don't have a care
Flaunting and showcasing for people to see
Acting like more than you will ever be
When deep down you're miserable and lonely
Needing to be more than you and you only

REPRIEVE

My eyes are dry
I weep no more
My heart is light
Troubles out the door
My plate now empty
Pain I no longer store
I'm past the need
To settle the score
Time has been my enemy
Love has made me grieve
But I'm starting a new chapter
Hurt, no longer an incurable disease

RESPECT

Respect is something that has to be earned
And cannot be demanded
Respect is part of a give and receive system
You give it and you shall receive it
Respect is something you should feel privileged
To give and honored to receive
None of us are born entitled to respect
But we all have the ability to become worthy of respect
Respect is obviously not understood and yet
So hungrily sought after
There is a clear meaning behind the issue of respect;
So many want it and so few are willing to give it
Too many of us do not understand that what you do not
Give you rarely, if ever, will receive
This is a give what you expect to receive world

ROUNDED FLATS

Up and down they go straight out
Over and under rolling without
Bending a thought in an ongoing mind
Counting street lines chasing time
Circling window seals blocks we call panes
Twisting totally free dodging acid rains

RUNWAY MODEL

She was very tall, so frail, and thin
Being that small should be a sin
She walks the runway with such grace
She has no personality, just a stoned pale face
She doesn't eat much, afraid of getting fat
Purging what she does, so nasty, no tact
She smiles for the cameras, putting on a show
Scared of what people would think if they did know
She hides her problem to stay at the top of her game
She can't tell anyone, so embarrassed, so ashamed
While she's on stage she prays not to bobble
She has to live this way to be
A RUNWAY MODEL

SALVATION

If we look long enough, we will find problems
And even less ways to help us solve them
We worry so much about what is wrong
Instead of living for the day, like we don't have too long
If we abandon our problems and embrace our families
We wouldn't worry so much about what might be
We would enjoy ourselves and remember those times
That we sat down together, laughed, and dined
Forever the world will have its share
Of things going wrong, we just have to care
We've all been given a standing invitation
To HIS eternal love and SALVATION

SHADOW ASSAULT

You crept into my world and changed my life
I never saw your face but I felt the knife
You stripped me of dignity and tore open my soul
You killed my spirit and emptied a heart that was whole
You forced my free will in your twisted game
You left me on my back lying in shame
But I gathered the strength to rise to my feet
I refused to lie down and allow you defeat

SHATTERED GLASS

When I found out
I didn't know how to react
I was stunned at first
And then I was hurt
I couldn't understand it
I didn't want to try
I felt as if I could lie down
Curl up inside myself and die
My memories had been distorted
My heart was crushed
Everything I knew was right
I had now learned was wrong
So many tears I cried
Through long and sleepless nights
You tried to make me feel guilty
With bitter verbal fights
I have to move forward and let go of the past
But first I must pick up the pieces of myself
Repairing the shattered glass

SILENT SUFFERING

He was polite and showed he cared
But was treated as if he wasn't there
He did what was asked without a word
Even if he though it was absurd
When no one else would, he stepped in
To do what was needed, to make a friend
He ran nonstop, no thanks at all
No one there for him, not even a call
He often wondered why he was not liked
Why people would do things to him out of spite
He couldn't read minds and would not pry
But know they would like him if they'd just try
He goes against his best judgement defiantly
Doing what they ask of him, suffering silently

SOLITUDE

I wish they would just leave me alone
When I don't want to talk
I have to get away, breathe, take a walk
The thoughts in my head are more than I can stand
Maybe someone else can figure them out better than I can
I don't want to share them though, my troubles are my own
They often have me feeling helpless and alone
I want to reach out but feel that I must
Stay to myself because I'm the only one I can trust
They don't understand and ask for my reasons
My mind they're trying to infiltrate, it feels like treason
People don't understand, they try to intrude
But I must insist on my solitude

SPELLBOUND

Reaching out for something to hold
Digging around through life like a mole
Gathering events from the garden of life
Plucking memories from the ones that run twice
Sniffing the air for endings without stench
Swallowing the rain with a thirst to quench
Heat from the sun that's eager to tell
How the lessons of life have you under a spell

SPITT

Disgusted with your lies
Strong contempt for you
Half the man I expected
Your dishonest heart knows no truth
Nauseous with your family
Big appetite for the streets
Your envy for adulterers
Why did life let us meet
Your flirtations with other women
And pleasures in what you do
Will make sure that what you throw out
Will come back to haunt you

STALKER

It lies with me at night to sleep
It wakes with me in the morning to eat
It views my thoughts before I can
It's visible to me but it's not human
It forces me to relive my past
It reminds me that any moment can be my last
It's the worst enemy of any kind
It's my very own Mind

STARTING OVER

Taking for granted your life with me
Living as if you want to be free
The sadness deep within my heart
Intensifies knowing we'll soon be apart
It costs so much for me to stay
It'll cost even more if I don't break away
I'm spinning around inside of me
Wondering why all this has to be
I've come to a point where I've fallen down
And getting up will prove to be a battle
With more than one round

STATISTICS

We meet and greet
Spend time and tweak
We date and mate
Love and procreate
We build and grow
Put on a show
We cherish then destroy
Lie and deploy
We fight and force
An inevitable divorce

STRANGE ENCOUNTERS

Looking as if they can see right through me
What is it that they're trying to see?
Our eyes would often meet
But tongues refused to speak
Without a sound there was silence
Not even my heartbeat
Without movement we were still
Is it my soul they seek?
Me guessing what this all meant
Them staring with unknown intent
My eyes tired but I dare not blink
If I lose focus, into my mind they will sink
They can't read me though, for only I hold the key
To the voyage through my mind
To be shared in my own time

STUCK ON A CRAYON

Though you and I have never passed on the street
You seem to have strong dislike for me
You've never said hello and allowed me to oblige
Because we're different by what you see on the outside
We're not that different though, you and I
We both pray to the same man up high
You base your ignorance on teachings of the past
How long will this stupidity last
Because what you see is only the color of socks
Or two of the many we find in a box

TAKE A WISH

Take a wish and make it yours
Believe that it will open doors
Trust that things will go your way
And make it happen everyday
Follow your dreams with an open heart
With trust in yourself from the start
Show yourself the things you can do
And that wish you took will soon come true

TAKEN FOR GRANTED

The sun and rain
The moon and stars
The slide on the playground
The monkey bars
The water we drink
The food we eat
The friends we have
The people we meet
The crisp night air
In life our pair
The sky above
The thing called love

TAPESTRY

I started out as a beautiful vision
I was of great importance at first
I was twisted, looped, and pulled
After a while, I was set aside
Eventually, you remembered I was there
Over time I had become tangled and knotted
Oh the trouble I'm now causing you
It's taking much to get me back to my previous state
Finally, the light at the end of the tunnel
I show my potential beauty again
You spend a lot of time with me
I'm again a priority
There's repetitive winding by you to me
I'm now complete
What a beautiful sight I am

TAYLOR

She seems angelic
Her beauty dominate
Her words innocent
Her heart pure
Her patience learning
Her skin baby soft
Love in her eyes
Her helpfulness evident
Her knowledge vast
Her age so young
A gift from god
Heart plentiful like water
She is my daughter

TEACH ME NEW

Teach me new
The things that were lost to you
Teach me new
The things that are tried and true
Teach me new
The places you've been
Teach me new
The old ones you call friends
Teach me new
The journey back home
Teach me new
And I'll never be alone

TEARS OF REASON

We cry when we're happy
We cry when we're sad
We cry during good times
We cry during bad
We cry at our birth
They cry at our death
We cry when the world takes
And we believe there's nothing left
Throughout the times, for countless years
We've shown our feelings through flowing tears

TEMPERAMENT

With the brisk night winds all my troubles blew away
I was a different person with the light of day
I stopped feeling so tortured inside
My feelings I no longer had to hide
The rough periods in my life have gone
They're no longer with me, no longer part of my home
My life, I treasure every single minute
Keeping happiness and love prominent within it
I feel safe enough to now take chances
Not living in unforeseen circumstances

TESTIFY

I was walking alone, deep in thought
Going over all the things I had been taught
I didn't know what was right anymore
I feel as if I've walked through a door
That is taking me places and opening my eyes
I think my whole life has been a disguise
In see so much now and understand it all
I'm no longer walking into brick walls
I feel as though my lungs have been opened
I can breathe now, the word has been spoken
I'm no longer confused, things have been clarified
And I feel as though now I can testify

THANKFUL

You may not realize it but it's true
I've searched this subject through and through
The greatest gifts in life are free
But can be taken for granted so easily
The love your spouse has for you
The children you hold dear and true
The favor that was asked of you with "please"
Your neighbors watching out for thieves
The friendly smile from a passerby
The sun shining bright in the sky
The friendly call just to say hi
Not knowing if it's your last goodbye
The grocery clerks greeting you by name
Their positive attitudes staying the same
Cherish everything and never have greed
Because nothing in life is guaranteed

THE INVINCIBLE MAN

I am invincible, I can't be touched
There is no law for me, I have far too much
I tell numerous lies and steal from friends
If I don't get caught, there'll be no end
I buy jury verdicts and politicians
I buy my women, in addition
I run illegal businesses and live by greed
If I continue this way, no one I'll ever need
I don't have a conscience, my heart is black
I can't be human, because a soul I lack
I do what I want because I can
I call myself, the invincible man

THE LITTLE THINGS

You bought me medicine when I was sick
My hands were cold and you gave me your gloves
Even though they didn't fit
The grass was high you mowed the lawn
I got home late my bath was drawn
The gas was low you took my car
The lid was too tight you opened the jar
My back was hurting you swept the floor
Before I could do it you opened the door
I was running late I didn't have time
You sat yours aside and ironed mine
I was feeling low and not like me
You held my hand and told me you loved me

THE MIRROR

I dreamed I woke up in a field
It felt so strange, so unreal
The sun was soft, the breeze was cool
I felt alone, lost, and confused
I don't know how I got to this place
My heart was pounding as if I were running a race
I looked around but could not see
No people, no houses, only me
I walked a while and came to a cliff
I became petrified, nervous, and stiff
I turned to run and as things became clearer
I wasn't asleep; I was standing in the mirror

THE OTHER DAY

The other day I got bad news
I thought I was going to die
I realized I couldn't change it
I started to scream and cry
Why is this happening?
It can't be true
There's been a mistake
This is me, not you
Where did I go wrong?
This can't be right
I feel so angry
I want to fight
I won't settle for this
I deserve a stay
From the bad news I got
The other day

THE OTHER MAN

This is about the other man
I try and see him whenever I can
He gives me that something I'm missing at home
Filling me up when I'm feeling alone
When we touch it's indescribable
The feeling I get is undeniable
I know what I'm doing is wrong
I have a husband, a family, a home
I want him so much he's hard to resist
If I want to keep my family I must insist
If nothing else, I want him as a friend
But it's hard to let what we have end
I have to do it; I'll try hard as I can
But I can't stop thinking about the other man

TIME

Ask me how I'm doing and I'll tell you how I feel
Put out your hand for me and I'll show you I am real
Ask me how it began and I'll tell you from the start
Show me that you love me and I'll freely give you my heart
Ask me what I'm thinking and I'll tell you what's on my mind
Sit down and talk to me, give me a little of your time

TIME WASTED

Why didn't you just treat me right
You had me wondering day and night
If I weren't enough for you
Why didn't you end it, just say we were through
I tried to talk, to tell you my side
You ignored my every word, just letting it ride
I knew right then I had to let go
I had to save some dignity, even as a show
I ignored your messages and changed my number
My time on you I would no longer squander
But now I see the tables are turning
You no longer have me and now you're yearning
For another chance to be with me
You had a good thing and now you see
That what's your loss is another's gain
And now you're starting to feel the pain
That I felt when you treated me bad
You made a mistake and now feel sad
I can't however, shed any tears
I've cried enough throughout the years
Now I see there's a world out there
With someone for me, with whom I can share
The things I gave and you tossed aside
Your promises will no longer tide
I now know that we were not meant
Though I have no regrets
My time could have been better spent!

TORMENTING DREAMS

They provoke your thoughts
And interrupt your night
They suspend your time
And capture your mind
They open the black hole
And drop you in
They circle your body
Against them you can't defend
They hold you in sleep
And torture your spirit
They inflict painful memories
And make you relive them
They release their restraints
And open your eyes
Giving you your sight
Never to forget that night

TRUE LOVE

I believe in true love as everyone should
It hurts, it cries, and sometimes it's good
There is no true love without some pain
Lord knows because when he cries it rains
When love is good it can be so much fun
Heaven lets us know this through the warm bright sun
When god puts us together we form a pact
He intends for us to keep his blessing strong and intact
When gods great gift is set asunder
He shows his displeasure with roaring thunder
When the two of you are right you'll fit like a glove
Proof positive there is a such thing as true love

TRUST IN HIM

Even when things seem at their worse
I trust in him that there is no curse
Even when I'm ready to throw in the towel and give up
He reminds me that nothing in life is easy and that's what
Makes me tough
When it seems bad things only happen to me
He reminds me to keep him first and to believe
I often wonder "why me"?
He opens my eyes and helps me to see
Through the bad times and the good
He reminds me things are, as they should
Even in my darkest hour when things seem most grim
He reminds me that all I have to do is trust in him

TRUTHFUL
EXAGGERATIONS

I love you more than life itself
For the love of your heart I'll give up all wealth
You are my sun, my moon, and stars
To be with you I'll fight in any wars
Without your love I cannot breathe
Without you in my life there is no need
Without you here there is no me
Without your sight I cannot see
Without your world as part of mine
I'm forever lost in space and time

TWO SPIRITS

I'm split between the two of me
Searching for what my eyes can't see
Fighting with me to gain control
Of this troubled and tortured rebel soul
Trying to merge to become complete
In this mortal body without sanity

WAKE-UP CALL

Something seemed just not quite right
She felt it down deep in her bones
It wasn't something she was aware of
But something she should have known
He tried so hard and tricked them all
But his time has come to take a fall
His fool has come out of her shell
And booked his seat on a flight to hell
Her time has now come in the game
To put him and his lies to shame
She made her move and came out ahead
The fool she played is finally dead!

WANNABE

Have you ever had the chance to see
Someone you would call a wannabe
They talk so much about having this and that
While class and etiquette they obviously lack
They always talk about having so much
They go on and on about their life and such
You hate to see them but try and be nice
What you really want to do is give them some advice
When you see them coming you give each other a tug
There she goes, where are my earplugs
You're so very lucky if you never meet
One of those, you know, a WANNABE

WE ONLY HAVE TODAY

People say it was just his time
And that we'll all be just fine
That doesn't ease or take the pain away
Nor does it keep my mind from going astray
I cried and cried until there were no more tears
I took for granted the time he was here, lost all those years
That taught me that tomorrow is not a given
So we should take time with our family, start living
I missed out on so much and shared so little
My spirit now is broken and brittle
I wish I could turn back the hands of time
To tell my father I love him one last time
Take this as a warning; don't miss out on an important date
To tell the people close to you how you feel before it's too late

WEATHER THE STORM

I know he still loves me, why can't he see
I'm still the same person I used to be
If he would only give us a chance
I know we can rekindle that special romance
There's been a lot of hurt and constant pain
But the kind of love we have, we can easily sustain
We've lasted through ups and downs
Good times and bad
While everything else was lost, true love we still had
I know we belong together, his heart is just torn
We can last through anything, we can even
Weather the storm

WINDS BLOW BACKWARDS

Like snow in summer
Moon in morning
Rain in desert
Chaos calming
Shadows in shade
Trees that bend
Water that's dry
Days with no end
These are confusions
That makes us stagger
Trying to move forward
While winds blow backwards

WINE WITH DEATH?

They picked the place and time for me
And came with escort so promptly
They hovered around to make sure that I
Didn't miss my ride without alibi
They locked me in where my dress was lay
To put on my ending the proper way
They walked me through time where I took my last glance
At what was my life and circumstance
I made it through and the last thing for me
Was to choose red or white with eternity

WISER

You turned your back
My things I packed
You went astray
My love, I took away
You led me wrong
Now you're all alone
You said you needed to live
My forgiveness, I cannot give
It broke my heart
But I chose a new start
There's nothing left to say
For me, it's now a new day

WOLVES

With intense eyes and mysterious grandeur
They walk the forest, their homes, with splendor
With their demeanor they can say so much
Impressing upon me the need to touch
Their coat of fur with ease and care
Allowing me a part of their world to share
A gift for me would be to walk amongst them
Learning their habits, forming a trust
Everything about them is beautiful to me
I want them around me they help to feed
My inner desires to be rid of worries
To walk in innocence, no troubles, no hurries
They represent that part of me
That would like to let go and just be free

WOMAN TO WOMAN

Woman to woman
Why are you trying to wreck my home?
Is it because you screwed yours up
And now you're alone?
Woman to woman
You don't know me... so why do
You badmouth me behind my back?
Is it because respect for yourself or
Any other woman you lack?
Woman to woman
Why do you buy when you can't afford?
Is it because having it
Makes you feel like something more?
Woman to woman
Is there a reason why you do what you do?
You know it's wrong...do you think it won't
Come back to you?

WRINKLES

Like broken concrete in the road
A telling part of my soul
Like cracks in a porcelain doll
Happiness in life temporarily stalled
Like the ease of life hard earned
Desperate lessons of the past learned
Like the crowding of my space
All showing the true nature of my face

7 E V E N

Seven days of the week
Seven nights no sleep
Seven mornings I rise
Seven lies analyzed
Seven dreams I live
Seven sins I forgive
Seven memories I forget
Seven strangers never met
Seven lives gone astray
Seven nevers come into play

X

Extenuating circumstances
That cause
Extreme emotions
Forcing me to
Expect the worse
And in doing so
Exposing all of myself
While trying to
Extract my thoughts
From the
Exotic places in my mind
So I can
Exonerate my feelings
From the
Experiences of life
And
Extend time with my soul

COMPLICATIONS AND IMAGES OF LIFE

We try so hard to do our best
But the world is like a never-ending test
We make the grades to just get by
While filling ourselves with lie after lie
We see life the way we want it to be
While blinding ourselves to reality
In justifying the wrong that we do to each other
We've created a cloak that conceals and smothers
The blackness we hold inside our hearts
Keeping us divided and worlds apart
We need a medium ground without strife
While dealing with the complications and images of life

THE PERFECT LOVE

It is honest
It is helpful
It is kind
It is gentle
It is warm
It is simple
It is true
It is patient
Always open
Never complacent
Hard to resist
It does not exist

About The Author

Kathleen was born in Bartow, Florida to the late John Lincoln Taylor of Mississippi and Anester (Ann) Hall of Winterhaven, Florida. Kathleen's parents moved to Vicksburg, Mississippi with six of her siblings in 1973 when she was two months old; she is the seventh of ten siblings, two brothers and seven sisters. Kathleen and her siblings were raised in Vicksburg where she met and married her soul mate and best friend, Anthony Bennett Sr. They have two teenage sons, Sheann and Anthony and a daughter Taylor.

CPSIA information can be obtained
at www.ICGtesting.com
Printed in the USA
BVHW030207141119
563818BV00001B/29/P